G000153763

Other 'crazy' gigglebooks by Bill Stott

Sex – it drives us crazy!

Marriage – it drives us crazy!

Football – it drives us crazy!

Cats – they drive us crazy!

Middle Age – it drives us crazy!

Golf – it drives us crazy!

Published in 2007 by Helen Exley Giftbooks in Great Britain

12 11 10 9 8 7 6 5 4 3

Selection and arrangement copyright © 2007 Helen Exley
Cartoons copyright © 2007 Bill Stott

ISBN: 978-1-84634-134-2

Edited by Gayle Morgan and Helen Exley

Printed in China

Helen Exley Giftbooks, 16 Chalk Hill, Watford, Herts, WD19 4BG, UK
www.helenexleygiftbooks.com

A HELEN EXLEY GIGGLEBOOK

Computers

THEY DRIVE US CRAZY!

CARTOONS
BY BILL STOTT

"Try plugging it in, Gerry...."

"Erm. You **have** done this before, haven't you?"

"And by the time I've listened to all the tunes I've got stored on this baby, I'll be 127 years old!"

"Can't read. Rarely speaks. Won't wash. But does have the highest score on Urban Deth Sqwad."

"Anyway, we'd better shut up. They're back."

"Hi Ben? You know all that stuff about computers talking to each other? Well, your RSTO keeps calling my MT301 a geek."

"Difficulties? Yes, I'm having difficulties!"

"You know, sometimes I get really nostalgic about actually meeting someone and talking to them...."

"And to save time reading all those boring reports, the printer is routed straight to the shredder."

"And this is the CD which explains how to use the manual. To play it, consult the manual."

"That's Penrose. He's a legend around here. Actually uses all his hand held's functions!"

"Sobering thought isn't it - how did we get by last month without the real time visualization capability?"

"Yes! She does have repetitive strain injury – but only because she makes so many mistakes that she has to key in everything at least half a dozen times!"

"Quadband, operates on 850/900, 1800/1900 MHZ, GSM/GPRS wireless networks - allows international roaming and makes a really neat door wedge."

"The program's user-friendly enough, but some of the programmers leave something to be desired...."

"This new system we've installed is capable of millions more mistakes than the old one...."

"Oh no!
I'm getting
laptop thigh!"

"Perhaps you'd like to talk to my laptop.
It's a lot more interesting than I am."

"Look – I'm sorry – please don't go blank –
I didn't mean to say you were stupid…."

"Video conferencing is fine, but not when we have adjacent desks...."

"There have been lots of cut-backs...."

"Yes! And I love you too XR/372, but please
be careful, someone might hear you...."

"That's the trouble with these older models – it's having a mid-life crisis...."

"Then she pointed out that my new P/K 470 didn't have asynchronus/synchronous operation capability. Did I feel stupid!"

"And, of course, another attractive feature of the MX7 is that it makes very fine toast."

"Frankly yes - there are things it can't do... Iron. Have babies. Dog walking. Embroidery. Hang gliding...."

"And would you believe in the basement they've got an ancient RK504? Wow, that baby must be three years old!"

"Then, with the G64 MK.III,
things get really interesting...."

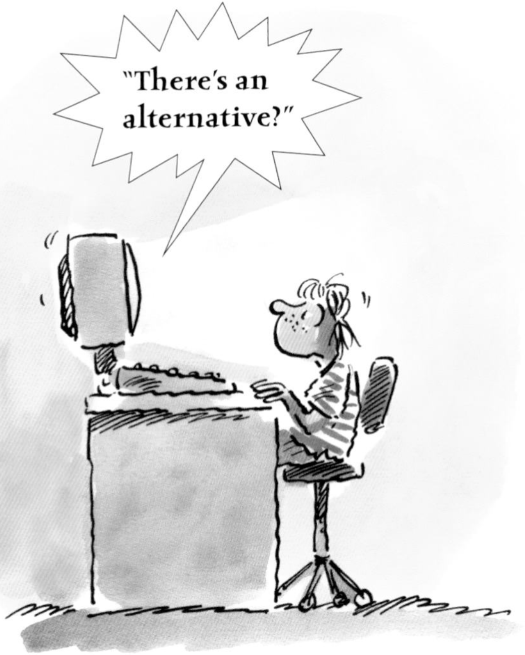

2

"Goodness Darren – what have you said to it? It's never done this before..."

"You've never really liked computers, have you, Grimsdale?"

About Bill Stott

Bill Stott is a freelance cartoonist whose work never fails to pinpoint the absurd and simply daft moments in our daily lives. Originally Head of Arts Faculty at a city high school, Bill launched himself as a freelance cartoonist. With sales of over 2.8 million books with Helen Exley Giftbooks, Bill has an impressive portfolio of 34 published titles, including his very successful *Spread of Over 40s' Jokes* and *Triumph of Over 50s' Jokes*.

Bill's work appears in many publications and magazines, ranging from the *The Times Educational Supplement* to *Practical Poultry*. An acclaimed after-dinner speaker, Bill subjects his audience to a generous helping of his wit and wisdom, illustrated with cartoons drawn deftly on the spot!

What is a Helen Exley giftbook?

We hope you enjoy *Computers – they drive us crazy!* It's just one of many hilarious cartoon books available from Helen Exley Giftbooks, all of which make special gifts. We try our best to bring you the funniest jokes because we want every book we publish to be great to give, great to receive.

HELEN EXLEY GIFTBOOKS creates gifts for all special occasions – not just birthdays, anniversaries and weddings, but for those times when you just want to say 'thanks' or make someone laugh. Why not visit our website, www. helenexleygiftbooks.com, and browse through all our gift ideas?

ALSO BY BILL STOTT
Marriage – it drives us crazy!
Cats – they drive us crazy!
Football – it drives us crazy!
Sex – it drives us crazy!
Golf – it drives us crazy!

Information on all our titles is also available from
Helen Exley Giftbooks, 16 Chalk Hill, Watford WD19 4BG, UK
www.helenexleygiftbooks.com